FAMOUS LIVES

The Story of
ALEXANDER GRAHAM BELL
Inventor of the Telephone

FAMOUS LIVES

titles in Large-Print Editions:

FAMOUS LIVES

The Story of
ALEXANDER GRAHAM BELL
Inventor of the Telephone

By Margaret Davidson
Illustrated By Stephen Marchesi

Gareth Stevens Publishing
MILWAUKEE

For a free color catalog describing Gareth Stevens Publishing's list of high-quality books
and multimedia programs, call 1-800-542-2595 (USA) or 1-800-461-9120 (Canada).
Gareth Stevens Publishing's Fax: (414) 225-0377.
See our catalog, too, on the World Wide Web: http://gsinc.com

Library of Congress Cataloging-in-Publication Data

Davidson, Margaret, 1936-
    The story of Alexander Graham Bell: inventor of the telephone /
by Margaret Davidson; illustrated by Stephen Marchesi.
       p. cm. — (Famous lives)
    Includes index.
    Summary: A biography of the man whose curiosity and perseverance led to
various inventions, particularly the telephone, for which he is best known.
    ISBN 0-8368-1483-5 (lib. bdg.)
    1. Bell, Alexander Graham, 1847-1922—Juvenile literature. 2. Inventors—
United States—Biography—Juvenile literature. [1. Bell, Alexander Graham,
1847-1922. 2. Inventors.] I. Marchesi, Stephen, ill. II. Title. III. Series:
Famous lives (Milwaukee, Wis.)
TK6143.B4D38   1997
621.385'092—dc21
[B]   97-586

The events described in this book are true. They have been carefully researched and
excerpted from authentic biographies, writings, and commentaries. No part of this
biography has been fictionalized. To learn more about Alexander Graham Bell, refer to
the list of books and videos at the back of this book, or ask your librarian to recommend
other fine books and videos.

First published in this edition in North America in 1997 by
Gareth Stevens Publishing
1555 North RiverCenter Drive, Suite 201
Milwaukee, Wisconsin 53212 USA

Original © 1989 by Parachute Press, Inc., as a Yearling Biography. Published by arrangement
with Bantam Doubleday Dell Books for Young Readers, a division of Bantam Doubleday Dell
Publishing Group, Inc. Additional end matter © 1997 by Gareth Stevens, Inc.

The trademark Yearling® is registered in the U.S. Patent and Trademark Office.
The trademark Dell® is registered in the U.S. Patent and Trademark Office.

Printed in the United States of America

1 2 3 4 5 6 7 8 9 01 00 99 98 97

Contents

Aleck's First Invention

Aleck and his friend Ben were having a wonderful time. They were out in the country, beyond the city streets of Edinburgh, chasing each other all around the rambling flour mill that Ben's father owned. They dashed from one storage shed to another. Then, laughing and shouting, they tumbled into the yard.

They must have been making too much noise. Suddenly Ben's father was standing in front of them, and he wasn't smiling.

"Can't you boys do something useful?" Mr. Herdman snapped.

"What would you suggest, sir?" Aleck asked.

For a moment Mr. Herdman's glare hardened.

But he could see that Aleck wasn't trying to be smart. The boy really wanted to know. So Mr. Herdman scooped up a handful of wheat. He explained that each kernel of grain was covered by a dry husk. In the 1850s it was not easy to separate the husk from the grain. "If you can figure out a practical way to get these husks off, it would be a real help," he remarked.

Aleck's eyes sparkled. When he went home that evening, one of his pockets was full of wheat. For days he tried one thing after another to get rid of those husks. First he simply rubbed the kernels between his fingers. Some of the husks came off, but some didn't. Doing it this way, his fingers were soon scratched and rubbed raw. Next he tried soaking the grain in a bowl of water. But that only turned the grain to mush. Finally he found an old nail brush that belonged to his father. He scrubbed a handful of grain with it, and the troublesome husks came off at last. But a brush for cleaning fingernails wasn't the answer, either. It was too slow and too small. No, what he needed was something much faster and bigger. Something more *mechanical*.

Then, suddenly, Aleck remembered the old machine he'd seen sitting forgotten in one of Mr. Herdman's sheds. It was shaped like a big barrel and it was open at the top. Inside, attached to a center pole, were a number of flat wooden boards like paddles. When the pole was turned, the paddles spun round and round.

Now what if you lined the inside of that barrel with rows of bristly brushes? Aleck wondered. What if you threw in a sack of grain and got those paddles spinning round and round? Then maybe, just maybe, the wheat would be flung against the brush and the husks would be scrubbed off.

Aleck explained his idea to Ben's father. At first Mr. Herdman had a funny look on his face, a look that plainly said, "Boys have such crazy ideas!" But Mr. Herdman was a fair man. He gave eleven-year-old Aleck's idea a try. And it worked!

Aleck remembered that happy moment for the rest of his life. Years later, when the world knew him as Alexander Graham Bell, inventor of the telephone, he said, "Mr. Herdman's suggestion that I do something useful led to my first successful invention."

As a young boy, Aleck was always curious. He loved to wander and to wonder about things. One of the places he liked to go was Corstorphine Hill, not far from his home in Edinburgh, Scotland. He would climb right to the top of the hill and then lie on his back in his favorite grassy spot, which he called "Rest-and-be-thankful." From there he could look down on the bustling town of Edinburgh or look up at the birds in the sky and set his imagination free. Oh, how he wanted to be up there with the birds—soaring, swooping, gliding, diving. People couldn't fly, of course. But maybe someday a machine would be invented that could fly.

"In boyhood, I spent many happy hours lying there dreaming such dreams among the heather on that Scottish hill," Alexander Graham Bell later remembered, "breathing in the scenery with a quiet delight."

But Aleck didn't spend all of his time dreaming. He also had a passion for collecting. He collected butterflies and insects, flowers, stones, birds' eggs, and interesting leaves. He carefully arranged them all on trays in his bedroom and created his own museum.

Aleck was especially proud of his animal bone collection. He had many bits and pieces of small animals, like toads and mice. He also had a complete cat skeleton, which a friend had found one day. But his pride and joy was a gift from his father, a human skull!

Aleck's mother didn't like that skull at all. His "piles of bones" gave her the creeps, she confessed more than once. But she never thought of telling

Aleck to get rid of them. That wasn't the way the Bells did things.

Aleck was born on March 3, 1847. He was the second of three sons. At that time, most parents had strict rules about raising children. They thought children should be seen and not heard. They expected children to obey without question. But Aleck's parents were unusual people. They set very few rules. And they encouraged their children to explore new ideas and new ways for doing things.

Aleck's father, Alexander Melville Bell, was a well-known elocutionist, a teacher of speech. He helped with stuttering or other speech problems. Professor Bell had a deep, clear voice. He was also a fine actor. Often, he gave public performances of the works of Shakespeare or of a modern English writer named Charles Dickens.

Aleck's mother, Eliza Bell, was talented as well. She was a very good artist. Many people came to her to have their portraits painted. She was a fine musician, too, and this was a talent Aleck shared. Often he sat at the piano and played for hours. Sometimes the melodies would ring in his mind, keeping him awake for most of the night. His mother called this "Aleck's musical fever."

Eliza thought so much of her son's talent that she

hired the best music teacher in all of Edinburgh to give him lessons. Monsieur Auguste Benoit Bertini agreed with Mrs. Bell. This promising youngster, he predicted, might one day grow up to be one of the leading concert pianists in all of Europe.

His whole life long, Aleck would never lose his love of the piano, but it was another trait of his mother's that most shaped Aleck's life. In addition to being a talented artist and musician, Eliza Bell was partially deaf. Professor Bell's work as an elocutionist combined with Eliza Bell's deafness resulted in the Bell family's unusual interest in many aspects of music, speech, and sound.

The Bells were not always serious. They had a lot of fun together. Several evenings a week they would gather in the parlor. Mr. and Mrs. Bell would play duets together—he on the flute, and she on the piano. Aleck's younger brother Ted would sing along in a clear tenor voice. Sometimes the music would be classical. Just as often they'd sing rousing Scottish folk songs. That's when Aleck and his older brother Melville ("Melly" for short) would join in singing at the top of their lungs.

The boys had other ways of amusing the family. Melly liked to imitate people. And Aleck had his own special game to make the others laugh. He'd pretend he was an angry bee, being chased around

17

the room. He'd dart and prowl around the parlor, mimicking perfectly the increasingly furious buzz of a bee.

There was no doubt about it. Life in the Bell household was a grand one for a growing boy as active and curious as Aleck. He didn't even have to go to school! Unlike other families that could afford to send their sons to school, Eliza Bell taught her children at home.

When Aleck was ten years old, though, the Bells decided it was finally time for him to get more formal schooling. Every weekday morning from then on, Aleck trudged off to school like everyone else. And suddenly life was a lot less fun.

"I Will Teach This Boy to Think!"

Aleck didn't hate school. He just didn't like it very much. He didn't like sitting quietly at a desk all day. He didn't like memorizing all those facts and dates. Most of all, Aleck didn't like studying things he thought were not going to be of any use to him, like Latin and Greek. Why should he have to learn dreary dead languages that nobody spoke any more?

History and geography didn't interest him much, either. Sometimes English was all right. He did like to read, and he had a definite talent for writing poetry. But all those rules of grammar and spelling—they were so dull.

Until now Aleck had spent most of his life doing

exactly *what* he felt like doing, *when* he felt like doing it. Now that someone else was telling him what to do, he didn't want to work very hard. He never failed anything, but he never got very good grades. For the next four years he simply coasted along.

Aleck's mother and father did encourage him to study more. But they knew their son was bright, and they didn't worry very much. One person in the family who did worry was Aleck's grandfather who often came from London to visit the family.

Aleck and his grandfather shared the same name and the same birthday. For one birthday, Aleck wrote his grandfather a poem. One verse read:

> Your birthday and mine are the same.
> I want to inherit your mind,
> As well as your much-honored name.

To inherit a mind was one thing, Grandfather Bell told Aleck's parents; to use it was another.

Grandfather Bell was an elocutionist, like Aleck's father. He was also a scholar, who passionately loved learning for its own sake. He decided it was time to do something about Aleck's education. So in 1862, at the age of fifteen, Aleck went to live in London for a year with his grandfather who was determined to teach him to *think*!

20

First, Grandfather Bell told Aleck that a gentleman, no matter how young, should be properly dressed. Aleck's rough tweed jackets and baggy old pants were hung in the back of the closet. In their place, Aleck was forced to wear skintight trousers and a fancy fitted jacket which choked him. When he went out he had to put on a top hat and gloves. Worst of all, "I have to carry a *cane!*" an outraged Aleck wrote his parents. Grandfather Bell's efforts to change the way Aleck dressed were all useless. For the rest of his life, Alexander Graham Bell would hate fancy clothes.

Grandfather Bell's attempts to educate Aleck were more successful. He taught Aleck to speak more clearly by having him recite Shakespeare's plays. He also encouraged him to master difficult subjects like ancient history, government, and English composition. But by far the most important thing Grandfather Bell taught the young Aleck was the value of education. Education, he said, was vital to a life well lived. He told Aleck that education was a ladder, a way of climbing out of ignorance and poverty. "Look at me," he said. "I started life as a simple shoemaker." But because of all the things he had studied and learned through the years, Grandfather Bell had risen to become a highly respected professional. Ignorance, Grandfather

Bell continued, was a crime because it isolated people, separating them from their own thoughts and stopping them from sharing their thoughts with others.

Aleck listened closely to his grandfather's words, and little by little something caught fire inside him. Before long he was studying harder and harder, trying to catch up with all he'd missed. He spent long hours in his grandfather's library and read all the books on language and sound. Now, instead of being a pianist, Aleck began to think about a career in speech.

"That year with my grandfather was the turning point in my whole life," Alexander Graham Bell wrote almost half a century later. "It converted me from a heedless boy into a man."

Soon after his sixteenth birthday, when Aleck was ready to return home, Professor Bell came to London to meet him. Together, they visited a man who, twenty-five years earlier, had made a "speaking machine." This machine couldn't actually speak, but it could imitate certain simple words and phrases. The man showed it to Aleck and his father, and when they got home, Professor Bell challenged Melly and Aleck to make their own machine. After reading a book about it, the boys agreed to try. Professor Bell cleared out half of the attic for them to use as a laboratory. Then he warned his sons that the task before them would take longer and be much harder than either of them could imagine.

He was right. First Aleck and Melly had to read a number of books to learn about all the parts of the body that went into making speech—the lips, the teeth, the tongue, the roof of the mouth, the throat, the windpipe, and the lungs. Before long their minds were whirling with technical words like soft palate, larynx, and pharynx.

Aleck and Melly kept at it, however, and slowly they began to make sense of the complex physical actions that lead to speech. Finally it was time to start building the model. The boys called it the "Little Man."

The brothers divided the work. Melly was responsible for the lungs, windpipe, and throat. Aleck was to make all the parts of the head and mouth. They faced many problems along the way. What material would they use? They wanted to make each part as lifelike as possible, but they could not use real skin or bones or nerves! This meant they had to experiment a great deal.

Melly finally decided to use an organ bellows for the lungs. He made the throat out of very thin tin and the windpipe out of a rubber tube.

Aleck wove together thin wires to make a frame for a head. He covered the frame with a skin of soft rubber, stuffed with cotton to form the cheeks. The lips were also made of wire covered with rubber. The roof of the Little Man's mouth was a piece of hinged wood.

The tongue gave Aleck the most trouble. It couldn't be too hard or too soft. It had to move in many directions at one time but still be all one piece. Finally Aleck decided to make the tongue, with carefully shaped wooden sections. Each section could be raised or lowered by pulling a separate string the way a puppet works. He padded the sections with cotton and then covered them with a thin sheet of rubber.

Finally, after months of effort, the Little Man was finished. Nothing remained but to try it out. It was hot in the attic that day. So Aleck and Melly carried their creation out into the hall. The brothers looked at one another, and each took a deep breath. The moment of truth had arrived.

Melly squeezed the bellows-lungs. Air rushed up through the tin throat. Aleck pulled the strings that moved the tongue. But only one sound came out. It was "ahhhhhhhhh." Then Aleck opened and closed the rubber lips very fast and another sound emerged. It was "mmmmmmmmm." Again and again those two sounds rang out in the hall. "Mmmmmm-aaaaaaa! Mmm-aaaAAAAA!"

The Bells lived in a large apartment on the top two floors of a house. Another family lived on the ground floor. Suddenly the downstairs neighbor threw open the door to her apartment and cried, "My goodness, what's the matter with that baby? Can't anybody stop it from crying?"

Aleck and Melly could barely hold back their laughter. The Little Man did sound exactly like a baby crying "Mama!" But the boys soon stopped laughing. After months of grueling work they'd managed to make just one little word. They felt their grand project was a total failure.

Their father didn't agree. He was very proud of his sons. They had made a machine that imitated human speech! They had also learned exactly how the different organs of speech worked and how they worked together to produce spoken words. But most important, they had learned a lesson that could not be measured by immediate success or failure. They had learned to pursue a project and to stick with it no matter how difficult it was. This was a lesson Alexander Graham Bell would recall many times in his life.

Sixteen-year-old Aleck was having a good time, but he was growing restless at home. The year he had just spent with Grandfather Bell had "given" him "a taste for independence," he later wrote. Aleck thought his father treated him like a young boy. Mr. Bell didn't even give his son an allowance. Aleck didn't like this a bit. He decided to do something about it.

First he thought of going to sea. He even had his bag packed and a ship picked out. But at the last moment he decided that this might be showing a little *too* much independence. Instead, he and Melly, who was also eager to be on his own, decided to get jobs. Day after day they studied the "Help Wanted" column in the local newspaper. At first it was discouraging. There were plenty of openings for cooks and handymen and baker's assistants. But what about something for two sons of a professor? Then, finally, they saw just the thing. A school named Weston House Academy, on the northern coast of Scotland, was looking for teachers of speech and music. The match was perfect! Melly could teach speech, since he already had public speaking experience. Aleck, who was still a fine piano player, could teach music.

The brothers sat right down and wrote a letter offering their services. It must have been a very good letter, for they soon got one in return. They were hired!

Aleck's father quickly heard about this example of budding independence. Not only had the boys used their father's name as a reference, but Professor Bell knew the principal of the Academy, who was responsible for hiring them! Professor Bell was not pleased. He insisted that Melly go to the university because he was old enough. Aleck, though, would get his chance to teach—he'd take both jobs at Weston House!

So Aleck, still only sixteen years old, began to work. He knew that several of his students were older than he was, but he was careful not to let them know this. Before long, he discovered that he loved to teach. He was very good at it, too. He always tried to make things interesting and fun, if he could. More important, he always made a point of finding out a student's strengths instead of embarrassing him about his weaknesses. No wonder his students loved him so much.

Teaching was only one thing that made Aleck's teenage years so interesting. He was also involved in the interesting work of his father. In addition to being a teacher of speech, Professor Bell was also something of a scientist—a scientist of sounds. For years he'd been studying what he called the "anatomy of speech," the exact positions of the lips, teeth, tongue, and throat when any sound was

spoken. He had written down all these positions in a kind of picture alphabet. People could study one of Professor Bell's pictures, shape their mouth and tongue exactly as shown, and the proper sound would come out—even if they had never heard it before! Professor Bell called this Visible Speech. It was a universal alphabet of sounds.

In 1864 Professor Bell perfected his Visible Speech alphabet. At first, people weren't very interested. It might be fine for simple noises, they said, but there were some sounds so complicated that they simply couldn't be written down. The song of the nightingale, for instance.

Aleck's father knew his critics were wrong, and he decided to prove it with a demonstration. He rented a large auditorium. He placed advertisements in the local newspaper and printed colorful posters to tell people about the event. All this planning paid off. On the night of the performance, the auditorium was packed.

Aleck had always been fascinated by Visible Speech. He had quickly learned to read it and to make the right sounds. He happened to be home on vacation when his father asked for his help with the demonstration.

Professor Bell introduced Aleck and then dismissed him from the auditorium. Then he asked people from the audience to suggest unusual words or noises. He wrote them all on a blackboard using the Visible Speech alphabet.

The hall was soon echoing with laughter as members of the audience offered one peculiar sound after another. One man imitated the cackling of a hen as it laid an egg. Another played a tune on his bagpipe, a series of howls, wails, and whines. A third provided sounds from Sanskrit, an ancient language of India. And so it went. One person blew his nose. Another pretended to sob. All the while Aleck's father stood by the blackboard and wrote signs.

Finally the audience grew quiet and Aleck returned. It was time for *his* part of the show. He stared at the big crowd, and for a moment he felt nervous. He took a deep breath and looked at the symbols his father had written on the blackboard. Then slowly and clearly, he began to translate them back into sounds again—exactly the right sounds!

Only once did Aleck hesitate. Surely his father must have made some mistake on this one, he thought. The sounds written down made no sense to him at all. But the audience laughed and cheered as Aleck began. He did a perfect imitation of a man sawing wood!

Tragedy Strikes

Aleck's father's experiments with sound were only one area of science being studied at that time. The mid-1860s was a time of exciting discoveries. Scientists were just beginning to ask basic questions like "What is light?" "What is sound?" "What is matter?" Today these questions are easily answered by scientists, but back then they were not.

Many scientists were also beginning to explore the fascinating field of electricity. One discovery they *had* made was that electricity could be used for sending coded messages over long distances by the dot-dot-dash of the telegraph.

Because of his family background, Aleck was naturally interested in the science of sound. Now he became more and more intrigued by the field of electricity. Before long his letters home were filled with information about electromagnets and acids and batteries. Naturally, it occurred to him that the sound of a human voice might be carried over an electric wire. It was about this time that Alexander Graham Bell had his first thought about the invention that would make him famous: the telephone.

This truly was a high point in Alexander Graham Bell's life. Then, suddenly, tragedy struck.

At first Aleck's younger brother Ted was just tired, so tired that some days he could hardly drag himself from his bed. Often his head was hot with fever, or his whole body would shake with chills. He was losing weight steadily. But worst of all was his cough, which grew worse and worse each day. The doctor examined him, but could do nothing to help. Young Ted Bell had tuberculosis, a terrible disease of the lungs that had no cure.

The Bell family had always been close. They had always eagerly helped one another. But united as they were, they could not conquer this disease. Aleck was helpless, as he watched Ted grow weaker and weaker. Once he and Ted had played tag and king-of-the-mountain together. Now Ted could not even sit up in bed.

Aleck was sitting by Ted's side on the morning

in May of 1867 when he died. "He was just 18 years and 8 months old," Aleck later wrote in his diary.

Crushed by his brother's death, Aleck found it hard to work. He returned to London, where his parents now lived.

In the spring of 1868 a woman came to see his father. She ran a private school for deaf children and she had heard about Professor Bell's Visible Speech. She wanted to find out if it could be used to help deaf boys and girls speak more like hearing children.

Of course it could, Aleck thought as soon as he heard the question. If *he* could read and then reproduce all sorts of sounds he'd never heard before, so could they. What a wonderful idea! As the son of a mother who was partially deaf, Aleck understood what a terribly isolated life most deaf people were forced to lead. Because they could not communicate like other people, the deaf were often poorly treated.

Aleck was terribly worn out from long months of teaching and working on scientific projects. But he gladly volunteered to teach Visible Speech at the school for deaf children. This was the start of a lifelong interest and commitment.

His first four pupils were intelligent and cheerful

little girls named Lotty, Minna, Kate, and Nelly. But how to go about teaching them? Aleck recalled everything he'd learned about speech since he and Melly had experimented with the Little Man. First he sketched a profile, the side view, of a human face and throat on a blackboard. Then he rubbed out all of the parts of it except the lower lip, the tongue, and some of the throat. What was left were the bits of lines to make various Visible Speech symbols for sounds.

Next he helped the girls shape their mouths in the various positions suggested by the Visible Speech symbols. Before the very first lesson was over, they had each learned more than ten sounds. Before the end of the fifth lesson, they were actually saying words!

Little Kate was especially happy. She had been born deaf, and her parents had never heard her speak a single word. Now she spent all her free time practicing a complete sentence as a surprise present for her mother. "I love you, Mama. I love you, Mama."

As Aleck watched Kate's progress, he was filled with happiness—for Kate and for himself. He knew he had found something that he truly loved doing—teaching the deaf. This new career combined so many of his loves: his love of speech, his love of teaching, and his fast-growing love of children.

But just when Aleck's future seemed certain, tragedy struck again. This time it was Melly, Aleck's older brother, with whom he was so close. Like Ted, Melly was struck down by tuberculosis. He died in the spring of 1870.

At age twenty-three, Aleck was his parents' only son. Now they had reason to be worried about him, too. For months he'd been suffering frightening spells of exhaustion and "nasty headaches" that sometimes lasted for almost a week.

Finally he went to a doctor. The doctor gave him a stern warning. If Aleck stayed in London's damp and foggy climate, he might have only six more months to live.

Aleck's mother and father acted immediately. They had already lost two boys. They were determined not to lose a third.

Although there was no medicine to cure tuberculosis, a dry and sunny climate could sometimes help. Once, many years before, Professor Bell had lived for a time in Canada. He had friends there, too, and recently he had lectured in the United States and in Canada. He knew how good the climate was there. The family, he decided, would pack up and move to Canada as soon as possible.

This was a big step for the family to take. Professor Bell was very famous in Britain. Not many people in Canada or the United States knew of his work.

Aleck was not at all sure he wanted to move. For one thing, he didn't think he had tuberculosis. He thought he had just been working too hard. Besides, all his dreams were for a future in Scotland and England, not in some faraway land he had never seen before. But Aleck also understood the suffering his brothers' deaths had caused his parents. He knew he was all they had left. So finally, Aleck agreed to go.

In July of 1870, the Bells sailed away to begin a new life near the small Canadian town of Brantford in the province of Ontario. They bought a house high on a bluff overlooking the Grand River. Before long, Aleck found a place on the edge of that bluff where the grass was very soft. He called it his "dreaming place" and spent most of his time there reading or looking down at the miles of rolling countryside spread out below. It reminded him of Corstorphine Hill in Edinburgh.

The pure Canadian air began to work its wonders, and soon Aleck was well again.

Now he was restless. He began to take long walks, exploring the countryside around Brantford. On one of these walks he discovered that a Mohawk

Indian tribe lived nearby, and he soon had a few Indian friends.

Naturally, Aleck immediately became interested in the Indian language. He began to learn it, and he offered to write it down in Visible Speech, so that others could also pronounce it. This pleased the Indians, especially the head of the tribe, Chief William Johnson.

One day Chief Johnson invited Aleck to his home for a dinner of wild fowl and other native food. Aleck declared it delicious! It was clear that he considered the Indian people to be his friends. He appreciated their language and customs.

The chief decided to show Aleck how much he liked him by giving him a rare honor. He adopted him into the tribe and made him an honorary chief. The adoption ceremony was one Aleck never forgot. Years later he wrote, "The Chief took me into his private room and dressed me up in full Indian costume. I wore his buckskin coat with silver britches made from silver coins. . . . Upon my head was placed his hat of eagle wings and ostrich feathers— which brought my height up to nearly eight feet. Then, dressed in full costume and with a tomahawk in my hand, I stalked majestically into the room where all the guests were seated—frightening my mother nearly out of her senses!"

The Indians also taught Aleck their war dance, full of whirling, stomping, and shouting. For the rest of his life it would serve him well. Whenever something especially wonderful happened—something he just couldn't express with mere words—he would break suddenly into that dance, complete with whoops and yells.

Aleck had made some good friends in his new home. Once more, he was healthy and happy, enjoying life in a new country that he liked very much. The rest of the family was also becoming comfortable in their new home. Professor Bell's talents were in demand, and he had gone several hundred miles south to Boston, in the United States, to lecture on Visible Speech. Now the principal of the Boston School for Deaf Mutes wanted him to return and teach her staff how to use his alphabet of sounds.

Professor Bell wasn't interested in the offer for himself. But he knew that Aleck needed to find work outside the sleepy little farming town of Brantford. He offered his son the chance to go to Boston, and Aleck leapt at it. In April 1871, twenty-four-year-old Alexander Graham Bell went to live in Boston. Here he began the most creative period of his life.

*   *   *

Aleck was welcomed by the school's teachers and students with open arms. Before long, he was busier than he had ever dreamed possible. Word spread about this outgoing, talented young teacher and soon he was teaching in *several* schools for the deaf. He was also lecturing and writing magazine articles about the need for more communication between deaf and hearing people. He started a small magazine called *The Visible Speech Pioneer*. He became a professor at the newly formed Boston University, and he taught a steadily increasing number of private pupils.

One student who crept straight into his heart was five-year-old Georgie Sanders. Georgie was too young to go to a special school for the deaf, so Aleck designed a program just for him. Aleck took a glove, and on it he wrote the letters of the alphabet and a few often-used words. Before long the boy and the man could talk to each other by pointing to different parts of the glove. They called it their "magic glove."

Aleck also made a point of reporting anything interesting or exciting he saw during his daily travels—a monkey begging for pennies with a tin cup, a runaway horse and rider, a caged parrot talking to its mistress on a train. He described all this to Georgie, with the help of the magic glove

and the sign language of the deaf. Aleck wanted to fire Georgie's imagination with all the chatter and clatter of a world that he would never hear.

Aleck's days were filled to overflowing. Still, as usual, he found time for science and inventing. This was an interest he shared with one of the first friends he had made in Boston. Her name was Sarah Fuller, and she was the principal of the Boston School for Deaf Mutes.

"He often came to my house in the evening and worked on his experiments until past midnight," she remarked. "And sometimes even until two in the morning."

Aleck's scientific ideas still centered around the problems of the deaf. Once he said to Miss Fuller wistfully, "If only I could make a machine to write sound, just as it is spoken. If only I could make a machine to hear for these children!"

Miss Fuller looked into Aleck's face. She could see that this wasn't just a nice young man with a passing interest in science. She suddenly realized she was looking at someone with unusual talent.

"Someday you *will* invent something very wonderful," she said to him slowly. "I don't know what it will be. But I know you will be famous someday."

The only thing she didn't guess was how soon it would be.

41

Aleck Begins to Dream Big Dreams

For nearly thirty years, the world had been using the electric telegraph, invented by Samuel Morse. It had made a great difference in people's lives. They no longer had to wait for days or weeks while a horse or a train or a ship carried their words to another part of the world. Now it all happened in an instant.

But one thing was wrong with the telegraph. Too many people wanted to use it at the same time. Only one message could be sent over a wire at once. Often, people had to wait in long lines. Sometimes, when people were going on a trip, they sent telegrams telling friends or relatives when to expect them at the train station. When they pulled into the station, they found that *they* had arrived before the telegram!

But, what if there were some way to send more than one message at a time, on the same wire? What if there were a way to send ten? Or fifteen? Or more? Several people were already trying to find a way to do just that. They were trying to invent a "multiple telegraph." Now Aleck decided to try, too. He thought he had a new and better idea.

All his life Aleck had studied music and the science of sound. He knew that the sounds of music were just vibrations of the air, rapid back-and-forth movements of molecules. Fast vibrations make high sounds, and slow vibrations make low sounds. The speed of the vibrations is called pitch.

Aleck also knew that if something like a guitar string was tuned to a certain pitch and plucked next to a piano, the piano string of *exactly the same pitch* (exactly the same sound) would vibrate in return. This was called sympathetic vibration; the two strings were in perfect sympathy with each other. In a way, they "understood" each other.

Now, Aleck thought, what if a telegraph transmitter sent out a message of a certain pitch? And what if the receiver at the other end of the line picked up messages with only that exact same pitch? Then it ought to be possible to send many different messages along the same telegraph wire at the same time—as long as each was a different pitch.

Yes! Aleck was sure of it! If only he could figure out the mechanical details, the idea would work. But when was he going to find the time? His days were filled with teaching and lecturing and all his other work for the deaf.

It would have to be at night, then. Aleck didn't mind working at night a bit. Since he was a child in Edinburgh, he had always had trouble falling asleep. Everything was so quiet and peaceful at night, it was the perfect time to think.

So Aleck worked away happily on his idea for developing a multiple telegraph. Before long his room was littered with transmitters and receivers and electromagnets. Slowly but surely he progressed toward his goal.

Then one afternoon he happened to be in the Boston Public Library. The library had just received a book called *The Wonders of Electricity*, and Aleck flipped through its pages. Suddenly he stopped, for his eye had been caught by a fascinating sentence. Using electricity, it said, "we may be able to transmit the vocal message itself with the very inflection, tone and accent of the speaker."

Aleck felt a jolt of excitement. This meant that, like Morse code, people's *voices* might one day travel over a wire to faraway places!

Before long, however, this first excitement began to fade. Aleck felt the same way he had felt when he and Melly built the "Little Man." What he read sounded exciting, but he soon realized that putting this idea into practice might well be impossible.

Through his experiments with the multiple telegraph, Aleck had already learned that electricity could be turned on and off many hundreds of times per second to make sounds of different pitches. But to transmit human speech, high and low pitch were not enough. Loudness and softness was required, as well. How could an on-and-off current of electricity transmit *that*?

It couldn't. To do that, the current would somehow have to change in *strength*, too. It would have to become stronger and weaker, just the way sound waves did as they traveled through air.

Such a current had never been made before. Was it possible? Aleck wasn't certain. He continued to think about these new ideas while he returned to his work on the multiple telegraph.

By the fall of 1874, Aleck wasn't just working for himself anymore. Two important businessmen had heard of Aleck's work on the new telegraph, and

45

they said they would be willing to pay some of the expenses for his experiments. One of the men was Thomas Sanders, the father of Georgie Sanders, the deaf boy who had learned to communicate with Aleck's "magic glove." Mr. Sanders was a wealthy leather merchant. The second man who was interested in Aleck's work was Gardiner Greene Hubbard, the father of another pupil, a deaf teenager named Mabel Hubbard.

Mr. Hubbard was a lawyer from a very wealthy Boston family. He had brought the first streetcars to Cambridge, Massachusetts; he was the president of Cambridge Gas Light Company; and he served for ten years on the state board of education. Later in his life, Mr. Hubbard founded the National Geographic Society.

Mr. Sanders and Mr. Hubbard were both used to success, and they believed that Aleck could bring them even greater success. They agreed to pay for any material he needed or any models he wanted to have built. In return they would become part-owners of the multiple telegraph invention, if and when it worked.

This was good news indeed. Up until now Aleck had made everything himself. But he wasn't very good with his hands, and it took far too long for him to make things. All too often he made such a mess of things that he had to throw out whatever he was working on and start over.

Now that he had some money, Aleck knew just where to go for the help he needed. The electrical workshop owned by Charles Williams, on Boston's Court Street, was *the* place inventors headed for when they wanted to get the best tools or to have models of their inventions made. In 1868 Thomas Edison had worked there.

It was a noisy, grimy place, bustling with about twenty-five skilled workers. Who was the best of the lot, Aleck wanted to know. Mr. Williams pointed to a corner where a thin young man sat hunched over a table. That young man was by far the brightest employee in the place, Mr. Williams told Aleck. He had a quick mind and always found ways to improve his work.

That sounded good to Aleck. So he walked over and shook hands with twenty-year-old Thomas Watson.

On the surface the two men seemed completely different. Aleck was very well educated. Tom had dropped out of school before he was twelve. Unlike Aleck, who was a perfect gentleman, thanks to his grandfather, Tom's manners were very rough. Until he met Aleck, Tom had never used a fork. Almost fifty years later Thomas Watson, then a

very well-known and successful man, wrote, "No finer influence than Graham Bell ever came into my life."

Despite their differences, Alexander Graham Bell, inventor, and Thomas Watson, his assistant, became partners in the truest and best of ways over the next few years. They were both the kind of people who asked "why" all the time. It was this shared curiosity that would keep them working together through all the disappointments and failures, until, finally, the moment of triumph, when the telephone was born.

"I Have Made a Discovery of Great Importance"

All through the winter and early spring of 1875 Aleck and Tom spent almost every evening together, experimenting on the multiple telegraph. They usually worked in the attic above Charles Williams' shop, after the other employees had gone home. Sometimes they worked at the home of Georgie Sanders' grandmother where Aleck lived, rent free, in exchange for teaching Georgie.

They worked with tuning forks, metal bars that could produce sounds with a definite pitch. The forks were arranged with a battery so that they turned those pitches into electrical signals.

Tom would sit at one end of a long room, a row

of tuning forks before him. At the other end of the room Aleck sat behind another group of tuning forks. A wire connected the two sets of forks.

Tom would make a sound with one of his tuning forks. Then Aleck, with his finely trained ear, would pick up one of *his* forks and listen to it—the one that was supposed to vibrate at the same pitch. Sometimes it did, but more often it didn't. Sometimes nothing happened at all.

Aleck was still sure that his basic idea was correct. But he couldn't seem to make it work in practice. No matter how carefully the forks had been tuned to each other, the notes sent along the wire usually wound up as a muddled mess.

Aleck was beginning to get more and more discouraged. One night he began talking to Tom about something else—something that might just be a crazy idea. What came spilling out, of course, was Aleck's dream for developing the telephone.

Tom Watson became more excited as he listened. It could work, he agreed. It could work *if* they were able, somehow, to make an electric current shaped like human sound waves.

Aleck nodded glumly. That was the heart of the problem. But what was the solution? This question was being asked by many others besides Aleck and Tom. Since the technology of the telegraph had been developed, many inventors and scientists had been experimenting with transmitting sound over electrical wires. One such inventor was Elisha Gray. Aleck was aware of the research Gray was doing in Chicago on the multiple telegraph and on machinery that could transmit the human voice. Gray, in fact, was one of Aleck's strongest competitors. Many people like Aleck and Elisha Gray understood the problems involved in transmitting the human voice but none, so far, had yet discovered the solution.

At the time Aleck first told Tom of his ideas for the telephone, he was busy getting ready to make a trip to Washington, D.C., to file for a patent on the multiple telegraph. He wanted to be sure none of his competitors claimed *this* invention.

While he was in Washington, Aleck paid a visit to a great American scientist. The man's name was Joseph Henry, and he was the head of the Smithsonian Institution, the center of science in America. Aleck wanted to tell the elderly physicist about his work and the problems he had been having with the multiple telegraph.

Professor Henry listened carefully and intently as Aleck talked. This encouraged Aleck so he also described the telephone. "I explained the idea and said, 'What would you advise me to do, publish it and let others work it out, or attempt to solve the problem myself?' "

Dr. Henry didn't hesitate. He said he thought the telephone idea was "the germ of a great invention." And with great excitement, he told Aleck to work on it himself.

These words, coming from such an important scientist, made Aleck feel wonderful. "But I am not really a trained scientist," he told Dr. Henry. "I'm a teacher. There are so many mechanical difficulties in the way. And I feel I don't have the electrical knowledge to overcome them."

Dr. Henry looked hard at the young man in front of him. Then he leaned forward, and he issued a flat order. "GET IT!"

"I cannot tell you how much those two words have encouraged me," Aleck wrote his parents a few days later.

Alexander Graham Bell needed every bit of encouragement he could find during the next several months. The multiple telegraph continued to pose problems. He was no nearer to finding the special kind of current he needed for his telephone, either. As he later wrote, "That spring of 1875 was indeed the dark hour just before the dawn."

Then came the night of June second. Aleck and

Tom were working in the attic of Williams' shop in two separate rooms. More than sixty feet separated them.

They were doing their usual experiments. But, now, steel organ reeds had replaced the tuning forks. A wire long enough to cover the sixty feet connected the reeds at either end.

Tom started one of his reeds vibrating. At the same time, he tuned it to a specific pitch by tightening a screw. Aleck, in the other room, held a receiver to his ear, straining to hear the vibrations. No sound came. Then Tom realized that the reed had become stuck. He flicked at the reed with his finger to free it, making a loud *t-waaannng* sound.

Suddenly Aleck jerked back in his chair. Then he gave a great shout and dashed into Tom's room. "What did you do?" he cried, his eyes gleaming with excitement. "Whatever it was, don't change anything! We've found it! We've found the current we want!"

Aleck later understood what had happened. Tom's jammed reed had stopped the usual strong on-and-off current from traveling through the wire. But it had caused another very faint current to be made. This current varied in strength exactly like the sound of the human voice! Again and again they tested their discovery. Again and again Aleck heard sounds carried by this new kind of current.

Aleck's special knowledge of music and sound was very important to that day's work. There were many scientists who knew much more about electricity than Aleck did, but no one else shared Aleck's unique background.

When Aleck went home, he couldn't sleep. As dawn began to turn the sky rosy, he sat down and wrote to one of the men who was backing him. "I have accidentally made a discovery of very great importance," he began.

The Telephone Is Born

What Aleck called his accidental discovery was of very great importance indeed. But there was still much work to be done before the telephone could become a reality, and Aleck knew it. "I am like a man in a fog who is sure of his latitude and longitude," he wrote his mother and father. "I know that I am close to the land for which I am bound and when the fog lifts I shall see it right before me."

The land might have been right before him. But for the next few months he made very little progress in getting to it.

One reason for this was that Tom Watson was sick. For weeks he was too ill to get out of bed. And

Aleck soon discovered that without this talented assistant, he could do very little work.

Besides, Aleck wasn't well himself. His problem was exhaustion, both of body and mind. He'd been working so long and so hard that even his seemingly endless enthusiasm wasn't enough to keep him going. Often he felt so tired he could hardly drag himself out of bed. And now his terrible headaches returned.

Another problem was money. He was paid for his work with the deaf, of course. But most of what he earned, he spent on his experiments. Mr. Sanders and Mr. Hubbard were paying for materials to build the multiple telegraph and for Tom Watson's services, but they were not paying Aleck for his work. "So I began to be in real want," Alexander Graham Bell remembered.

Mr. Gardiner Hubbard was especially upset that Aleck was spending so much time working on the telephone. Again and again he cautioned him to keep his attention focused on the multiple telegraph. "If you don't," Mr. Hubbard warned sternly, "you will be in danger of accomplishing nothing of value at all."

There was another reason why Mr. Hubbard wanted Aleck to work on a sensible project that he thought would be successful. Alexander Graham

Bell had somehow found the time to fall in love with his daughter Mabel.

Mabel Hubbard had lost her hearing as a child of five because of scarlet fever. From the first, her family had encouraged her to learn lip-reading and to continue speaking. But it was hard for many people to understand her blurred speech. Several years earlier, Aleck had been hired to teach her Visible Speech. Soon her voice became more clear and pleasing. And soon the teacher and pupil fell deeply in love. Aleck was now twenty-eight years old and he wanted to marry Mabel.

But Mr. Hubbard worried that Aleck—a man who seemed to have such impossible dreams—would never make enough money to care for his daughter properly. Finally, in the fall of 1875, Mr. Hubbard issued an ultimatum, a direct order. Aleck, he said, must choose either teaching and Visible Speech or inventions and Mabel. He said he would pay Aleck's living expenses if he chose Mabel and inventing.

Aleck showed that he could be very firm himself. "Should Mabel love me as devotedly as I love her," he wrote Mr. Hubbard, "she will not object to any work in which I am engaged as long as it is honorable . . . If she does not love me well enough to accept me, whatever my profession—I do not want her at all."

Mabel was barely eighteen years old. But she also knew her own mind. On November 25, 1875, her eighteenth birthday, they became engaged. Aleck wrote a letter home, telling his parents all about it, and he signed it, "Your happy son, Alec." From now on, Aleck would spell his name without the letter "k," the way Americans spelled it.

Tom Watson was finally well, and Alec was able to turn his attention back to the telephone. At first all he and Tom heard were faint gasping and sputtering sounds. But little by little things got better. One day Tom, who was listening in another room, came running in to say, "I heard your voice then! I could *almost* make out what you said!"

But faint echoes of words were not good enough. So the two men kept on trying. As usual, most of their work was done at night. This disturbed Mabel. She felt that Alec would become seriously ill from lack of sleep. "Please, please, please, for me, work fewer hours," she begged. Alec agreed to work in the day, but found he could not get anything done.

Finally Mabel got tired of pleading. For three days she disappeared into her room in the Hubbards' house. When she next saw Alec she had a package in her hand. "It's a portrait I painted of you," she announced. Alec was pleased and touched. But when he unwrapped the picture he threw back his head and roared with laughter. For Mabel had painted him the way she saw him, as a life-sized night owl with bright black eyes!

The new year of 1876 changed Alec's life forever. One of the first things he did was move his workshop from the attic over Charles Williams' shop. Too many workers there were becoming interested in what was going on. So he took two rooms in an old boarding house at No. 5 Exeter Place.

Alec had cause to be worried. Word of what he was working on *had* become known in scientific circles. Alec was a trusting man, but several times visitors to the shop had made him uneasy by trying to find out what he was doing. He guessed that Elisha Gray, the Chicago inventor, had sent them. Did they want to steal his ideas?

Mr. Hubbard was worried, too. Mabel's father still was not at all sure that the telephone would ever work. But little by little he had come to see that it might. And he knew that several other men were striving to develop the same thing. So he began urging Alec to get a patent on what he had discovered so far—so no one else could claim the invention.

But Alec had promised one of his parents' neighbors, a man named Mr. Brown, that he would not file for the patent yet. Mr. Brown had given Alec a little money. To repay Mr. Brown, Alec agreed to let him file for the British patent. It took time for Mr. Brown to get to England, and then he delayed filing the patent application, thinking people would laugh at the idea of the telephone. Meanwhile, Alec waited in the United States.

Finally Mr. Hubbard lost patience with Alec. He went down to Washington, D.C. and at ten o'clock on the morning of February 14, 1876, he filed the patent application himself. It was lucky Mr. Hubbard did. Just a few hours later, on that very same day, Elisha Gray, Alec's competitor, filed a sort of prepatent, called a caveat, for what he called a "speaking telephone." Mr. Brown never did file the British patent.

On March 3, 1876, the U.S. Patent Office formally approved Alec's telephone patent. It was his twenty-ninth birthday, and Alec noted that he received "a very nice present." Indeed it was. Patent No. 174,465 would turn out to be one of the most valuable ever issued from that day to this.

Although they had patented the basic idea, making it work was another story. Alec and Tom went on with their experimenting as usual.

A week later they were trying out a new transmitter that Alec had designed and Tom had just built. Neither of them was very excited about it. They had tried so many things. Some had worked better than others, but none well enough. This was just another experiment.

Alec sat quietly in one room, with his transmitter by his side. Tom, as usual, waited in a nearby room with a receiver pressed against his ear.

Alec leaned over his transmitter and began to speak in a normal tone of voice. Suddenly, in the other room, with two doors closed between, he heard Tom Watson give a great shout.

Moments later Tom came crashing into the room. "I heard you!" he was shouting. "I *heard* you And not just your voice. I heard *words*!"

Alec jumped to his feet. "What did I say? Repeat my words!"

Tom was stuttering with excitement. He stopped to take a deep breath of air. Then he continued more calmly. "You said, 'Mr. Watson. Come here. I want you.' "

Those seven simple words would change the world. It was March 10, 1876, and the telephone had been born.

"I Hear! I Hear!"

Alec, Mr. Hubbard, Mr. Sanders, and Tom Watson all hoped to share in money that a telephone company might earn. Now that the invention worked, they had to find a way to tell people about it.

Fortunately, there was a way. In 1876, there were many celebrations for the hundredth birthday of the United States. The biggest celebration of all was about to start in Philadelphia at the end of June. It was called the Centennial Exhibition, and inventions from many lands would be shown there. "You must go and let the world see your telephone," everyone told Alec.

But Alec refused. He said it wasn't ready. It

needed more work, more adjustments. Besides, he was too busy getting ready to give final examinations for his deaf students.

Maybe he believed all these excuses. Or perhaps he was just frightened. Whatever the reason, Mabel refused to listen to him. One afternoon she came by the school where Alec was teaching and said she felt like taking him for a drive. They went for a drive, all right, straight to the railroad station!

Alec protested. He said he couldn't show the telephone by himself. He needed an assistant, and Tom Watson was busy. Mabel pointed out that her cousin, Willie Hubbard, would do almost as well.

"I haven't got any clothes," Alec said. Mabel pulled out a small suitcase from under the carriage seat.

"No ticket," Alec sputtered. But he wasn't surprised by now when Mabel took a long white envelope from her purse. Ticket in hand, he boarded the train for Philadelphia.

The next day, Alec, still shaking his head with disbelief, set up his telephone equipment. Because he was so late he couldn't put it with the rest of the electrical exhibits. The only place left was off in a dark corner of the Massachusetts educational section which Mabel's father had helped organize.

On Sunday, June 25, the judging of electrical

inventions was about to begin. But what a hot day! Alec, as usual when the temperature soared, was just plain miserable. It was plain that the judges were, too. They had just spent a long time talking to Bell's main rival, Elisha Gray. His exhibit was sponsored by Western Union, at that time one of the largest companies in the United States. Alec watched the judges come closer and closer. He recognized two of the judges. One was Sir William Thomson, a famous English scientist. The other was Dom Pedro II, Emperor of Brazil.

Now the judges were standing by the exhibit right next to Alec's. He could hear exactly what they were saying. And what they were talking about was the weather. They were saying they couldn't stand any more of this heat. They were going back to their hotel rooms and would finish the judging tomorrow.

But he wouldn't be here tomorrow! He had to give final examinations in Boston the next morning. The trip would be all for nothing. When the judges finally looked at the telephone, there would be nobody there to explain how it worked.

Alec started to turn away. And then, as he liked to say later, "the miracle happened."

"How do you do, Mr. Bell?" a voice cried. "And how are the deaf mutes of Boston?" It was the

Emperor of Brazil, calling to him. Alec had met the emperor briefly just a few weeks earlier when Dom Pedro had toured the school where Alec taught. But Alec never thought the man would remember him.

Dom Pedro did remember him, and called the other judges over to meet him. When he discovered that Alec had invented something called a telephone, the emperor told the judges that they must examine it right then. The judges didn't look at all happy about this. But Dom Pedro was the guest of honor at the exhibition, so they did what he said.

The next few minutes passed in a blur for Alec. He explained how the telephone worked. The judges said nothing. One looked bored. Another plainly thought Alec was talking gibberish. But mostly they looked hot.

Alec cut his talk short and walked across to a transmitter, which he had placed at the far end of the hall. Then he motioned for Dom Pedro to pick up the receiver.

Alec began to speak. "To be or not to be," he said quietly. "That is the question . . ." He was reciting a famous passage from one of Shakespeare's plays into the transmitter.

For a long moment Alec waited. Then suddenly Dom Pedro exclaimed "I hear! I hear!"

After that, of course, the other judges nearly fell over each other trying to hear the machine that spoke. For three hours these men, who had been so eager to go home a few minutes before, listened and marveled at Alexander Graham Bell's invention.

"Gentlemen," Sir William announced, "this is the most wonderful thing I have seen in America."

The other judges agreed. Even Elisha Gray, who stood among the judges, thought Bell's invention was wonderful. When the Centennial Exhibition closed, Alec was awarded a first prize for his telephone.

After that, news of the telephone seemed suddenly to be everywhere. Long articles in important magazines like *Nature* and *Scientific American* were written about it. Learned societies like the British Association for the Advancement of Science lavished praise on it. No wonder people everywhere wanted to find out more about this new invention called a telephone. Alec received letters from everywhere. Once, he received eighty-three letters in four days!

For the next few months Alec and Tom Watson gave one demonstration after another. Alec had a lot of fun. He was a born lecturer and he loved being dramatic.

His audiences had fun too. Alec would rent a hall and rig up a telephone on the stage. Tom would be waiting at the other end of a telephone line back in Alec's rooms at No. 5 Exeter Place. "Hoy! Hoy! Mr. Watson," Alec would say. "Would you like to sing for us?"

And the audience would gasp as Tom's voice came booming out of the receiver, singing such rousing tunes as "Hold the Fort," "Pull for the Shore," and "Yankee Doodle." "My voice was terrible, but my singing was always a hit," Tom Watson later remembered.

Alec's landlady was the one person who didn't appreciate Tom Watson's voice. One night, after Alec and Tom had made the first long distance call from Boston to Cambridge, Massachusetts, they had celebrated with an especially loud war dance. The singing and dancing disturbed the other people living at Exeter Place, but it would have pleased the Canadian Indians who first taught Alec the dance. "If you don't stop making so much noise and keeping my lodgers awake, you'll have to quit them rooms," the landlady told Alec the next morning.

It was Tom who found a way around this. He got some pieces of wood and hung blankets over them to make a kind of tunnel. He did his singing from inside this contraption. "It was suffocating but soundproof," Tom said. It was also the world's first telephone booth!

While Alec was perfecting his telephone, he hardly had time to work with his deaf students. But they were never far from his mind, especially since Mabel had found a place in his heart. "I only wish, darling," he wrote Mabel, "that you could hear my instruments." Alec always thought of himself as a teacher. He planned to make enough money from his inventions to marry Mabel and continue what he saw as his real work: teaching the deaf.

On July 11, 1877, one year after the telephone was born, Alec and Mabel were married. On the day before the wedding, Alec handed Mabel a long envelope. She gasped as she read what was inside. It was a legal document that gave to her almost all the fortune that the telephone would bring.

Oh, Alec," Mabel said. "You are giving me *all of your future*."

"That is what I want to do," he answered.

And, indeed, use of the telephone was growing by leaps and bounds. "It reminds me of a child," Alec wrote, "only it grows much more rapidly. What is before it in the future, no man can tell—but

I see new possibilities ... and new uses all the time."

The Bell Telephone Company had officially been born on July 9, 1877. Its first customer was Charles Williams, the man at whose shop Alec had done so much of his early work. He ordered a line connecting his home with the shop. "I went into his office this afternoon," Alec wrote, "and found him *talking to his wife by the telephone* ... and they had no difficulty in understanding one another ... *the telephone is in practical use!*"

In February of 1878 the first telephone directory was issued. It listed eight names. Very quickly after that it was replaced by another. This listed eleven homes, three doctors, two dentists, twenty stores and factories, four meat and fish markets, two horse stables, the police station, and the post office.

Communication by telephone was becoming popular and the Bell Telephone Company was thriving. Then, suddenly, Alec and the company found themselves challenged.

The Western Union Telegraph Company had begun to manufacture and sell telephones too. Among its employees were Elisha Gray, Bell's early competitor, and Thomas Edison, who had improved Bell's transmitter. By combining the patents of these and other inventors, Western Union argued that it controlled the rights to the telephone. So it took Alec and the newborn Bell Telephone Company to court.

Alec knew that the Western Union charge couldn't possibly be true. He knew he'd been the first to develop the telephone. But the Western Union Company was a rich and powerful company. It had all the money it needed and more to hire teams of fast-talking lawyers. How could the new and tiny Bell Telephone fight such a giant?

Discouraged, Alec wasn't at all sure he wanted to fight. He was an honorable man, and Western Union's dishonesty and greed angered him. He thought about giving up his rights to the telephone. "The more fame a man gets for an invention," he wrote, "the more does he become a target for the world to shoot at. I am disgusted . . . so let others vindicate my claims if they choose. But keep me out of the strife." To his wife he added mournfully, "I have lost the telephone."

Alec announced that he'd decided to take up teaching again. And to Tom Watson he said firmly, "Will you please understand and believe that I am serious about this."

Tom tried to convince Alec that he *had* to fight. But Alec was stubborn.

He would not listen until Tom hit upon another

of his strong qualities, his sense of justice. Would it be fair to all the other people in the Bell Company if Alec just turned his back on the invention?

This question persuaded Alec to fight Western Union in court. The suit dragged on for over a year. And when it was over in 1879, he had won. Even before the verdict, Western Union knew they had lost. Alec's testimony was eloquent and impressive.

For the next eighteen years Alec's patents were tested in more than six hundred separate court cases. Alec and the Bell Telephone Company won every single case. This proved, beyond a shadow of a doubt, that Alexander Graham Bell was the one and only inventor of the telephone.

Alec Continues
Inventing

In 1878 Alec and Mabel moved from Boston to Washington, D.C. With them went their baby daughter Elsie, who had been born earlier that year.

Alec was busy as ever. He said, "Wherever you may find an inventor he will go on inventing. He can no more help inventing than he can help thinking or breathing."

Soon after the Bells settled in their new home the French government awarded Alec one of their highest honors—the Volta Prize for scientific achievement in electricity. A large amount of money came with the prize. Alec used it to set up the Volta Laboratory, a "permanent, self-supporting" place for scientific research. Before long he and a small team of assistants were working on an especially exciting project.

Another great inventor, Thomas Edison, had just developed the phonograph, but his design left much to be desired. For records, Edison's phonograph used cylinders that looked like cans of beans. They were clumsy, hard to store, and easily broken. They also had a very short playing time.

In addition, they could only be played a few times before they wore out. Worst of all, they couldn't be reproduced, so it was impossible to make more than one copy of a recording. Edison, himself, had lost all faith in the machine and had begun research on electric lighting.

But Alec and his team saw the phonograph differently. They developed an entirely new kind of record, one that was round and flat. It was easy to store, sounded much better, and had a longer playing time. Most important, other records could be made from it. With these improvements, the phonograph became popular. Before long it was a common household item. Some say this was the greatest invention of the Volta Laboratory.

Alec always said that "the inventor is a man who

looks around upon the world, and is not contented with things as they are. He wants to improve whatever he sees. He wants to benefit the world."

The summer of 1881 brought an unexpected opportunity for Alec's help. The nation was shocked when President James Garfield was shot in the back. The bullet didn't kill him right away, but the doctors couldn't find it, and day by day he grew weaker.

Alec set to work immediately developing an electric probe that could locate bullets lodged in the body. On July 26, Alec took his device to the White House and passed it over President Garfield's body. Unfortunately, the machine didn't work. Alec made another attempt, but this one failed too. Frustrated, he ran more experiments on his probe but, unfortunately, President Garfield was too weak for Alec to try again. Two months later, Alec grieved when President Garfield's death was announced. It was later found that the bullet lodged in the president's body was too deep to be detected by Alec's probe.

Despite this first failure, the electric probe did go on to be much more successful in other cases. Hospitals used it for many years and so did doctors treating wounded soldiers, until the X-ray was invented.

Another of Alec's medical inventions was the

"vacuum jacket." It was prompted by the death of Alec's newborn son of respiratory failure in the summer of 1881, just weeks before President Garfield's death. It was made of metal and surrounded a person from waist to neck. When air was pumped in and out of it, the patient could breathe more easily. It was an early kind of iron lung.

Not all Alec's inventions were successful. In the early 1880s he developed a different kind of telephone, which used sunlight instead of wire to transmit sound from one place to another. Alec called it the "photophone" and considered it his greatest invention, outranking even the telephone.

But few people agreed with him. After all, they pointed out, the sun doesn't always shine, so the photophone simply wasn't practical. This time, Bell's critics were right. Even today no use has been found for the photophone.

Honors continued to pour in. The French government made Alec an officer of the Legion of Honor and invited him to speak before their Academy of Science. In Germany, the University of Heidelburg was so impressed by "this American inventor," as they called him, that they made him an honorary Doctor of Medicine.

As a matter of fact, Alec *wasn't* an American yet. But on November 10, 1882, thirty-five-year-old

Alexander Graham Bell swore allegiance to the United States of America. He became a citizen of the country that had been so good to him for the past ten years. He always considered this the greatest honor of all.

By now the Bells had a second daughter, Marian, who was nicknamed "Daisy." In 1883 another infant son died. Sorrow over the death of their sons haunted Alec and Mabel for the rest of their lives.

Alec loved his family deeply. But the true center of his life was Mabel. "I dread absence from you," he wrote her when he had to be away on business. "It is NOT RIGHT. Let us stop it NOW. . . . Let us lay it down as a principle of our lives, *that we shall be together.*" Another time he added, "You have grown into my heart, my darling, and taken root there, and you cannot be plucked out without tearing it to pieces."

Mabel returned his feelings. "It is wonderful how I miss you the moment you are out of reach . . . my big burly husband. . . . You are the object around which all my life moves. Do take care of yourself, for I love you so very much."

Mabel knew all of Alec's talents and strengths, as well as his quirks and faults. She wasn't bothered, for example, by his morning routine. Alec always demanded the same exact breakfast, which he ate in a precise and unchanging way each day. His regular menu was one bowl of hot oatmeal with sugar, one bowl of chilled cream, two soft-boiled eggs, and coffee. First he would take one spoonful of oatmeal, then one of cream, and one of egg. He also insisted on drinking liquids through glass tubes and straws. It made perfectly good sense to him. "I want to put the liquid in my mouth, not my mouth into the liquid," he explained.

One of Alec's habits that Mabel still couldn't get used to was his working by night and sleeping by day. Again and again she scolded him, "I cannot bear to have people think you are doing nothing, and wonder what can you do if you don't work when others work? Please, please, if you love me, work in the daytime and not at night."

Alec tried. One night at their vacation home in Canada, he climbed up and down a steep hill behind the house twice, so he could tire himself out enough to sleep. But at three o'clock in the morning he was still wide awake. That night he wrote, "To take night from me is to rob me of *life*."

Another habit that Mabel disliked was Alec's love of solitude. She was very social, but Alec sometimes tried hard to avoid people. One afternoon they were supposed to visit some of Mabel's friends. Alec didn't feel like it, so he hid in the attic behind some rolls of carpet. Mabel soon tracked him down by the smell of his cigar, which he always smoked. "I will have to give up smoking," he moaned. "There is too much work to be done in the world for men to spend their time sipping tea from house to house!"

Many of Alec's activities still involved the problems of the deaf. "I am more sure every day," he wrote Mabel, "that my interest in the deaf is to be a lifelong thing with me. I see so much to be done—and so few to do it—so few *qualified* to do it. I shall never leave this work. So whatever successes I may meet with in life, your husband will always be known as a 'teacher of the deaf.' "

In a speech he gave in 1887, Alec tried to describe what it feels like to be deaf. "Who can picture the isolation of their lives? When we go out in the country and walk in the fields . . . we think we are solitary, but what is that to the solitude of an intellectual being in the midst of a crowd . . . with whom he can not communicate and who can not communicate with him."

One day Alec went to visit a school for the deaf. He had by now grown rather stout and wore a long bushy beard. "Some of the youngest children in the school somehow got the idea that I was no less an individual than Santa Claus himself!" he later re-membered.

Alec played along, and spent a happy few min-utes describing how he drove his team of reindeer over the tops of houses.

The children happily accepted this. But soon it became plain that they were puzzled by something. How could such a *big* body get down something as *small* as a chimney? "I taught them the word 'squeeze' so that they will never forget it!" Alec wrote. "I'm afraid that half of the school will write to me before Christmas and I shall have to visit the school in appropriate costume!"

Alec spent a great deal of his time writing, giving newspaper interviews, and talking before govern-ment committees about the deaf. He was trying to convince people that the deaf should be taught to speak so they could communicate with people in a common language. "For communication is what ideas, and friendship, and love are all about."

Alec wanted to find out if deafness could be passed along from one generation to the next. He became a pioneer in heredity research. By studying family histories, he found that when two deaf people marry, the chances of them having a deaf child increases. Alec's work became so important that his Volta Laboratory was renamed the Volta

Bureau and it became a center for information on the deaf. Today, the Volta Bureau is a historic landmark building that is the home of the Alexander Graham Bell Association for the deaf.

One day in 1887 Alec was sitting in his office when his secretary told him that a mother and father were waiting outside with their deaf daughter. They had traveled all the way from Alabama to see him.

It was the end of the day and Alec wanted to get home. But how could he turn his back on such need? "Never turn a child away," he cautioned again and again. "And never ignore their questions. They may be seeing something we adults have overlooked."

When the family came in, Alec studied the little girl. She was about six years old with wild-looking eyes and tangled hair. The girl's father told him she had been blind as well as deaf since the age of nineteen months.

Alec reached out and lifted the child onto his knee. For a long moment the girl just sat there. Then she, too, reached out, wrapped her arms around his neck, and snuggled against him.

"But Helen doesn't do that!" her mother gasped. "She never lets anyone but her family touch her!"

The little girl was Helen Keller. She would grow

up to be respected and loved by people everywhere for her brave fight to conquer her disabilities. But right now her world was lonely and empty. She would always remember the day when she first met Alexander Graham Bell. "He understood me," she wrote later. "And I knew it and loved him at once. He was my first friend."

After a while, Helen slipped from Alec's knee and began to explore the room. She examined every object she could reach with her curious hands.

"I believe that your little girl is very intelligent," Alec told the Kellers. "And I believe she can be educated."

Alexander Graham Bell had looked beyond Helen's differences and seen a real and whole child there. He recommended that the Kellers get in touch with the Perkins Institution for the blind, in Boston. "They will be able to find a teacher for Helen," he said, gathering her in his arms once more.

"And so," Helen Keller wrote years later, "my teacher came to me." This teacher was Anne Sullivan Macy, the woman who freed Helen from her loneliness.

Writing again of Alexander Graham Bell, Helen said, "I loved him at once. But I did not dream that

that interview would be the door through which I should pass from darkness into light, from isolation to friendship, companionship, knowledge and love."

Alec, Helen, and Anne were to be lifelong friends. "When others doubted, it was you who heartened me," Helen Keller wrote him many years later. "You have always shown a father's joy in my successes and a father's tenderness when things have not gone right."

One day, many years after his death, when she met one of Alec's granddaughters, Helen told her, "I am still hungry for the touch of his dear hand."

"Mr. Watson, Come Here, I Want You."—Again

As the years passed, Alexander Graham Bell had less and less to do with the daily work of the fast-growing telephone company that bore his name. As he said, "The lonely, fascinating pioneer work" of the early days was over. He was a scientist, not a businessman. Tom Watson, the man who had heard those first seven words spoken over an electric wire, felt the same way. In 1881 he, too, quit the company to travel and follow a path of self-education. For a time he owned one of the largest shipyards in the nation.

Alec was very happy living in Washington, D.C.,

and working on new projects there. Only one thing about the city bothered him; the weather. Being in Washington during the summer, he complained, was like living in a pot of hot soup. Being Alec, of course, he set out to try and change the climate.

One blisteringly hot day a reporter met him on the street. Was Mr. Bell working on something new? he wanted to know.

Alec's eyes twinkled. Well, he *was* experimenting with something, he answered. He suggested that the reporter come by his house later to see it.

When the reporter arrived, Alec led him toward a swimming pool that the Bells had just built in their backyard. But he hadn't brought a bathing suit, the reporter protested. Alec assured him he wouldn't need one. There was no water in the pool.

When they got to the edge of the pool, the reporter blinked with surprise. At the bottom was a furnished room, including a rug, desk, lamp, and two comfortable chairs.

As they climbed down into the "room," the reporter got another surprise. How cool it was! he exclaimed.

Alec nodded. That was his experiment, he explained. Up in the third floor bathroom he had put a big box filled with chunks of ice. Then he had placed an electric fan next to it to blow air over the ice. The cooled air flowed into a canvas fire hose which hung down the outside of the house, and ended up inside the pool. Alec had invented an early kind of air conditioning.

· But he could not spend all his time at the bottom · of a swimming pool. He and Mabel began to look for a summer home where they would be more comfortable. Before long they found exactly what they were looking for, on Canada's Cape Breton Island. It was a place of ocean and lakes, blue skies and cool winds, sunny meadows and steep hills. Everything, Alec said, reminded him of his happy boyhood in Scotland.

The Bells bought hundreds of acres of land on the edge of a bay. There they built a big, rambling house. They named it "Beinn Bhreagh," meaning Beautiful Mountain in Gaelic, the Scottish language. Right behind the house there rose a steep hill. Like Corstorphine Hill in Scotland and his "dreaming place" in Brantford, Canada, this was Alec's favorite place of all.

From 1893, for almost thirty years, Beinn Bhreagh was Alec's vacation home. But it was also much more. As usual, Alec's curious, restless mind was bubbling with experiments and inventions waiting to be born. Before long, the whole place became another one of his laboratories.

There he worked on a great number of projects. To help save shipwrecked sailors, he developed a machine that made salt-water fresh. He bred sheep, an experiment in heredity, to see if they could bear more than one lamb at a time. He suggested an echo device for measuring the depth of water, and another device for detecting icebergs in the dark. He and his assistants built what was then the fastest motorboat in the world. And for more than twenty years he experimented with flying machines.

Out of this last work he developed something called tetrahedral cells. Each cell had four triangular sides and was extraordinarily strong, yet light. Today, space frames, as they are now called, are used in all sorts of construction, from massive buildings to bridges stretching across broad rivers.

"Alec always saw something fresh and exciting, even in the most commonplace things," a friend summed up. "Wondering was almost a passion with him."

Alec poured a fantastic amount of energy into experimenting and inventing. But he worked almost as hard at having fun. "Everyone beat a path to their door," another friend remembered. "Something was always going on. Often they had as many as twenty-six house guests packed into their home."

Every August Alec and Mabel threw a gala cele-bration they called "Harvest Home." Friends and relatives for miles around were invited. All day long they ran races, flew kites, chased greased pigs, sang, and ate delicious food.

In the evening they all piled into one of the big barns at Beinn Bhreagh. First there were dramatic readings. Then Alec played the piano and sang for the audience. Everyone danced till dawn.

Alec thoroughly enjoyed his growing brood of grandchildren. Grampie, as they called him, was especially close to his oldest grandson, Melville Bell Grosvenor, born in 1901.

Melville's earliest memory was of sitting on his grandfather's lap and playing a special game. "I'd reach up and tweak his nose and he'd bark like a dog. Next I'd pull his hair and he'd bleat like a sheep. But the best of all was when I tugged on his beard. Then he'd throw back his head and growl fiercely like a bear!"

When he was a bit older, Melville read a book called *Robinson Crusoe*. It was about a man who was shipwrecked on a desert island and had to live entirely by his wits.

"Is it just a story, Grampie?" Melville asked. "Or can it really be done?"

Alec was a white-haired old gentleman by now. But he was as eager as ever to try a new experiment. So one day, he and Melville set off into the woods surrounding the Bells' Canadian home. They were dressed only in bathing suits, and they had no food or tools. This was part of the experiment. They had to survive without any of the trappings of "civilization."

The experiment was doomed to quick failure. Before long, a cold mist filled the air and set the two adventurers to shivering. The only things they found to eat were some seeds growing on weeds and a few berries. Their search for clothing was no more successful. For quite a while they tried to stick moss to their bodies with mud. But as the mud dried the moss dropped off in big chunks.

Finally Alec and Melville were forced to retreat to the warmth of the Bell kitchen, where they heated up a can of beans.

"Well, we did learn one thing," Alec, ever the teacher, remarked.

"What was that, Grampie?"

"We learned that Robinson Crusoe was a lucky man. *His* island was tropical."

As the years passed, Alec never stopped experimenting. He never stopped inventing, and he never stopped having a grand time. On January 25, 1915, when Alexander Graham Bell was 67 years old, the telephone again became the center of national attention.

For the past forty years, telephone wires had been run in every direction over greater and greater distances. Now they had finally been run all the way across the United States.

A great celebration was planned to commemorate the occasion of the first telephone call between the East and West coasts. A number of important people took part. The first call was to be made by the president of the United States to the governor of California. "Hello!" said President Woodrow Wilson from the White House. "I greet the great state of California from Washington, D.C.!"

Then it was time for the two *really* important men to speak to one another. Alec sat in an office in New York City. His face was lined and his beard was completely white by now. But his black eyes still sparkled. At the other end of the line, in California, waited Alec's former assistant and friend, Tom Watson.

Reporters had been asking Alec for days what he planned to say on this special occasion. But Alec refused to answer. "You'll have to wait and see," was all he would say.

Now it was time. Alec picked up his telephone and spoke first. "Hoy, hoy, Mr. Watson!" he said loudly. "Are you there? Do you hear me?"

Tom replied, "Perfectly, I can hear every word."

Alec paused. Then he said, "Mr. Watson. Come here. I want you!"

They were the same words he had spoken almost forty years before when the telephone was born. And Tom remembered them well. From three thousand miles away, he chuckled. "I'd like to, Dr. Bell," he answered. "But it isn't so simple *this* time. This time it would take me a week!"

A Wonderful Way to Say Goodbye

Alec was sixty-seven years old when that ceremony took place. For a number of years he'd been battling diabetes, an illness for which there was no cure. The only way to help control it was to stay on a strict diet.

Alec really tried hard to stay on his diet, but he loved to eat. One night, long after everyone else was asleep, he crept downstairs and cleaned out the icebox. After his midnight raid, he was careful to wash every plate and every piece of silverware. He swept up every crumb. But despite his efforts to cover his tracks, Alec was found out. Hours later a terrible stomachache brought the doctor to the Bells' front door.

"My God, sir, to load up on Smithfield ham, cold potatoes, macaroni and cheese, *and* apple pie! That is the most ridiculous thing imaginable. Why, that meal might have been the end of you, sir!" the horrified doctor cried when he heard what Alec had eaten.

Even now, sick as he was, Alec refused to lose his sense of humor. "Well, if it is," he whispered weakly, "the game was worth the candle. It was the best meal I've enjoyed in an age."

For the next few years, Alec tried to ignore his illness. As usual, he kept on working. "There cannot be mental decay," he said, "if a person continues to observe, to remember what he observes, and to seek answers for the hows and whys of things." And when anyone asked him how he felt, he would answer, "I never felt better in my life!"

Alec always looked ahead. Many people were urging him to write his autobiography, the story of his life, but he always refused. "I am as yet too much interested in the future . . . to give the time to a book of this character about the past," he said.

When he was seventy-five years old, Alec grew more ill. He became so weak, he could not leave his bed. Now he lay there, holding Mabel's hand, as he called for his secretary to take down a statement.

"Don't hurry," someone said.

"I have to," he answered. "I want to say that Mrs. Bell and I have both had a very happy life . . . And we couldn't have had better daughters . . . or finer grandchildren . . ." As usual, he was thinking of the people he loved best.

"Don't leave me," Mabel murmured. Alec's fingers clasped hers in the sign-language signal for "no." But a few moments later his curious and restless spirit was finally still. It was August 2, 1922.

Two days later he was buried on top of the mountain at Beinn Bhreagh, the Canadian home he loved so much. Mabel requested that only happy music be played during the service. "This is important," she wrote, "because his life was such a joyous one."

At the end of the ceremony, all the people bowed their heads in silence. At that moment, throughout the United States and Canada, every telephone that bore the symbol of Alexander Graham Bell's name also fell silent. It was time for the world to say its last goodbye to the father of the telephone.

ALEXANDER GRAHAM BELL

1847 On March 3, Alexander (Aleck) Graham Bell is born in Edinburgh, Scotland.

1858 Aleck produces his first invention — a machine that takes the husks off wheat.

1862 Aleck goes to London, England, to live and study with Grandfather Bell.

1863 Aleck and Melly build the "Little Man."

1867 Aleck begins his first job teaching school.

Ted Bell, Aleck's younger brother, dies.

1870 Aleck's older brother, Melly Bell, dies.

The Bell family moves to Canada.

1871 In April, Aleck moves to Boston, Massachusetts, to teach at the Boston School for Deaf Mutes.

1872 Aleck begins work on the multiple telegraph.

1875 In January, Aleck meets Tom Watson, and a great scientific team is born.

On November 25, Aleck and Mabel (Hubbard) are engaged to be married.

Aleck changes the spelling of his name to Alec.

1876 On March 3, the United States Patent Office approves a patent on the telephone.

On March 10, the human voice is carried over a telephone transmitter for the first time when Alexander Graham Bell speaks the words, "Mr. Watson. Come here. I want you," to Thomas Watson.

On June 25, the telephone is awarded a First Prize at the Centennial Exhibition in Philadelphia, Pennsylvania.

1877 On July 9, the Bell Telephone Company is officially started.

On July 11, Alec and Mabel are married.

1878 In February, the first telephone directory is issued. It lists eight names.

On May 8, daughter Elsie is born.

Western Union Telegraph Company goes to court, arguing that it, *not* the newly formed Bell Telephone Company, was the first to develop the telephone. Western Union loses the case in 1879.

1880   The French government awards Alec the
Volta Prize for scientific achievement in
electricity. With the prize money, Alec sets
up the Volta Laboratory.

On February 15, daughter Marian (Daisy)
is born.

1882   On November 10, Alec becomes a citizen of
the United States of America.

1887   Alec meets the Keller family. He helps them
find a teacher for six-year-old Helen, and she
and Alec become lifelong friends.

1915   On January 25, Alec and Tom Watson
commemorate the occasion of the first
coast-to-coast telephone call. From New York,
Alec speaks to Tom in California.

1922   Alexander Graham Bell dies on August 2.

For Further Study

More Books to Read

Aleck Bell, Ingenious Boy. Mabel Ross Cleland Widdemer (Bobbs-Merrill)

Alexander Graham Bell. Andrew Dunn (Bookwright)

Alexander Graham Bell. Patricia Ryon Quiri (Franklin Watts)

Alexander Graham Bell, Man of Sound. Elizabeth Rider Montgomery (Garrard)

Eureka! It's a Telephone. Jeanne Bendick (Millbrook Press)

Hello, Alexander Graham Bell Speaking. Cynthia Copeland Lewis (Dillon Press)

Telephone: Words Over Wires. Marcus Webb (Lucent Books)

Telephones. Gini Holland (Benchmark Books)

Videos

Alexander Graham Bell: The Telephone. (Barr Films)

Alexander Graham Bell: The Voice Heard 'Round the World. (AIMS Media)

Index